High–Frequency Picture Words
Literacy Skills Series

Written by Staci Marck

GRADE K-1

Classroom Complete Press

P.O. Box 19729
San Diego, CA 92159
Tel: 1-800-663-3609 | Fax: 1-800-663-3608
Email: service@classroomcompletepress.com

www.classroomcompletepress.com

ISBN-13: 978-1-55319-406-4
ISBN-10: 1-55319-406-3

© 2009

Critical Thinking Skills

High-Frequency Picture Words Grade K-1

Skills For Critical Thinking		Boxed Words	Mixed Up Words	Sentence Completion	Match and Print	Picture Word Match	Writing Tasks	Crossword	Word Search	Graphic Organizers
LEVEL 1 Remembering	• Identify	✓		✓	✓	✓		✓	✓	✓
	• Read	✓	✓	✓	✓	✓	✓	✓	✓	✓
	• Match	✓	✓	✓	✓	✓				
	• Select	✓	✓	✓	✓	✓				✓
	• Record	✓	✓	✓	✓	✓				
LEVEL 2 Understanding	• Use				✓		✓			✓
	• Describe									✓
	• Reorganize		✓							
	• Interpret			✓					✓	✓
LEVEL 3 Applying	• Choose Information			✓	✓		✓		✓	✓
	• Construct								✓	✓
	• Apply What Is Learned	✓	✓	✓			✓		✓	✓
LEVEL 4 Analysing	• Discriminate	✓	✓	✓	✓	✓		✓	✓	✓
	• Illustrate				✓		✓			✓
	• Identify Relationships							✓		✓
LEVEL 5 Evaluating	• Decide						✓	✓		✓
	• Make Choices			✓	✓	✓	✓			✓
	• Explain						✓			
LEVEL 6 Creating	• Design (i.e., a picture book)						✓			✓
	• Create						✓			✓

Based on Bloom's Taxonomy

Contents

• • • • • • • • • • • • • • • • • •

✔ **6 BONUS Activity Pages!** Additional worksheets for your students **FREE!**

• Go to our website: **www.classroomcompletepress.com/bonus**
• Enter item CC1114 or High-Frequency Picture Words
• Enter pass code CC1114D for Activity Pages

Assessment Rubric

• • • • • • • • • • • • • • • • • •

High-Frequency Picture Words Grade K-1

Student's Name: _____ Assignment: _____ Level: _____

	Level 1	Level 2	Level 3	Level 4
Picture Word Recognition	• Recognizes a few picture words	• Recognizes some picture words	• Recognizes most picture words	• Recognizes almost all picture words
Rhyme Awareness	• Recognizes when a few words rhyme	• Recognizes when some words rhyme	• Recognizes when most words rhyme	• Recognizes when all words rhyme
Identifies Beginning Sounds/Letters in Words	• Identifies a few beginning sounds/ letters of picture words (b – ball)	• Identifies some beginning sounds/ letters of picture words (b – ball)	• Identifies most beginning sounds/ letters of picture words (b – ball)	• Thoroughly identifies beginning sounds/ letters of picture words (b – ball)
Use the Shape of the Word to Identify it and Write it	• Uses a few letter shapes to identify and write words	• Uses some letter shapes to identify and write words	• Uses many letter shapes to identify and write words	• Always uses shapes to identify and write words
Sentence Creation	• Creates a few simple sentences that are slightly clear	• Creates some simple sentences that are moderately clear	• Creates many sentences that are usually clear	• Creates sentences that are extremely clear

STRENGTHS:

WEAKNESSES:

NEXT STEPS:

Teacher Guide

Our resource has been created for ease of use by both TEACHERS and STUDENTS alike.

Introduction

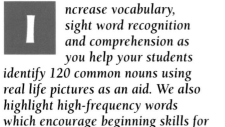

Increase vocabulary, sight word recognition and comprehension as you help your students identify 120 common nouns using real life pictures as an aid. We also highlight high-frequency words which encourage beginning skills for reading. As students begin to read and build their picture word knowledge, they will build a bank of known vocabulary words that will aid them in beginning to read and spell. Boxes are used to help students come to understand that words can be recognized by the shapes of their letters, as they contain small, tall or hanging letters. Reproducible worksheets are included for mixed up words, boxed words, writing, cloze sentences, and puzzles. This resource provides ready-to-use information and activities for beginning readers. It can be used in any Language Arts program as a supplement to a balanced literacy program to strengthen children's reading, writing and thinking skills.

Words are best learned in context. It is best to introduce the activities in this book as they appear in your shared reading, guided reading, writing and words blocks. Label the common nouns present in your environment to make student acquisition of picture words more seamless. This resource is comprised of interesting and engaging student activities in language, reading comprehension and writing, and can be effectively used for individual, small group or whole class activities.

How Is Our Resource Organized?

Activities in language, reading comprehension and writing (in the form of reproducible worksheets) make up the majority of our resource. There are a variety of pages organized in the following sections – BOXED WORDS activities, MIXED UP WORDS activities, CLOZE activities, MATCH AND PRINT

activities, PICTURE WORD activities and WRITING tasks. All are either a half-page or full page long.

It is not expected that all activities will be used, but they are provided for variety and flexibility in the resource.

- Flash cards are provided to help build student recognition of words. Reproduce them, cut them apart, mount them on a sturdy back and laminate. Make several sets in order to make games like "Concentration" and "Go Fish". Copies of flash cards could also be sent home to build student knowledge and understanding of picture words.

- Also provided are two puzzles, a word search and a crossword. Each of these worksheets can be completed as individual activities or done in pairs.

- Six Graphic Organizers are included to help develop students' thinking and writing skills. The Assessment Rubric (page 4) is a useful tool for evaluating students' responses to many of the activities in our resource. The Comprehension Quiz (page 48) can be used for either a follow-up review or assessment at the completion of the unit.

EASY MARKING™ ANSWER KEY

Marking students' worksheets is fast and easy with our **Answer Key**. Answers are listed in columns – just line up the column with its corresponding worksheet, as shown, and see how every question matches up with its answer!

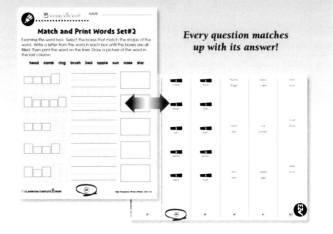

Every question matches up with its answer!

Before You Teach

1,2,3,4,5,6
Graphic Organizers

Suggestions for using the six **Graphic Organizers** included in our Picture Word Book are found below. They may also be adapted to suit the individual needs of your students. The organizers can be used on a projection system or interactive whiteboard in teacher-led activities, and/or photocopied for use as student worksheets. To evaluate students' responses to any of the organizers, you may wish to use the **Assessment Rubric** (on page 4). Once each activity has been taught and practiced many times, it can become a center or be used as an individual activity.

SOUNDS THE SAME

This organizer can be used as a whole class, small group or individual activity. To introduce this to the whole class, talk about rhyming words. Ask the students: How do you know when words rhyme? Do these words rhyme – boy/girl, bat/cat, fish/dish, cat/mouse? When you are confident that the majority of the students understand rhyming words, ask students to suggest picture words that they know. Create a list on the board of all the suggestions. Choose five words from the list that you can find rhyming words for. One at a time, orally manipulate each word to create real and nonsense words. Ask students to listen to each rhyming word: Does the word make sense? Does it sound right? Together determine if it is a real word. Record three real rhyming words for each picture word, then repeat the same process for the next picture word until the sheet is complete. **Found on Page 55.**

WRITE THE ROOM

This organizer can be used as a whole class, small group or individual activity. Ask students to look around the classroom for picture words. Together, brainstorm a list of picture words found in the classroom. Choose five words. Write one on each line and draw a picture to match each word. Write a sentence using three of the words. *At first, the group may need manipulatives to assist them with this activity. You could provide students with the vocabulary list from page 8 or the flash cards to help them identify picture words.* **Found on Page 56.**

USE THE CLUES

This organizer can be used as a whole class, small group or individual activity. For a class activity, lead your students through how to successfully complete this activity. Prior to beginning the activity, pick a picture word. Fill in the clues. Together brainstorm 3-4 possible answers to each clue in the side margin. Model how to eliminate guesses that do not fit the subsequent clues.

Extend the activity by having students write their own sentence using the word. **Found on Page 57.**

1,2,3,4,5,6
Graphic Organizers

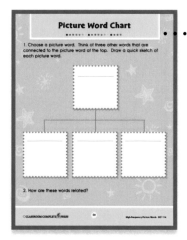

PICTURE WORD CHART

This organizer can be used as a whole class, small group or individual activity. Begin by demonstrating with your whole class how to complete this activity successfully. Prior to beginning the activity, pick a picture word. Show the students how to complete the organizer. For instance, if the picture word face is used, related words would include ear, eye and mouth. Demonstrate how to make a quick sketch of each word in the box with the word. Ask students how are these words related? They are all parts of the face. Model the process until students are competent then have students complete the activity in a small group or individual activity. Found on Page 58.

PREDICT THE HIDDEN WORD

This organizer is a whole class and/or small group activity. Place a sticky note on the picture words and pictures in the story. Read the title to the students and ask them what lives on a farm and what kinds of things happen there. Ask students to predict what word is hidden as you read the passage aloud. In the side margin record three student predictions for each word covered. Reveal one letter at a time for the covered words. As each letter is revealed:

- Do the predictions look possible (does the first letter match each predicted word?)
- Ask students if they would like to cross any out?
- Ask students if they would like to change their predictions, why or why not?
- Adjust words accordingly.
- Circle the word that matches the prediction as letters are revealed.
- Reveal the picture. Does the word match the picture?

Celebrate all of the words that the students accurately predict. Found on Page 59.

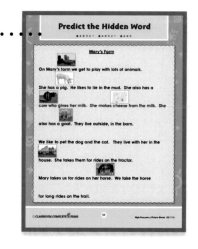

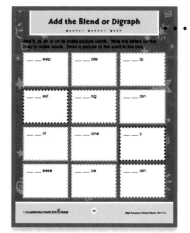

ADD THE BLEND OR DIGRAPH

This organizer can be used as a whole class, small group or individual activity. Begin by demonstrating with your whole class how to complete this activity successfully. Practice reviewing the blends and digraphs. Orally blend the blends and digraphs with the chunk or word ending. Ask: Does it make sense? Does it sound right? Does it look right? Once you identify the correct blend or digraph to add to the chunk or word ending, read the word together and model how to draw a picture to match the word. Model the procedure until students are competent with the activity, and then have students complete it in a small group or individually. Found on Page 60.

Bloom's Taxonomy* for Reading Comprehension

The activities in this resource engage and build the full range of thinking skills that are essential for students' reading comprehension. Based on the six levels of thinking in Bloom's Taxonomy, questions are given that challenge students to not only recall what they have read, but to move beyond this to understand the text through higher-order thinking. By using higher-order skills of applying, analysing, evaluating and creating, students become active readers, drawing more meaning from the text, and applying and extending their learning in more sophisticated ways.

Our **High-Frequency Picture Words Book**, therefore, is an effective tool for any Language Arts program. Whether it is used in whole or in part, or adapted to meet individual student needs, this resource provides teachers with the important questions to ask, inspiring students' interest, creativity, and promoting meaningful learning.

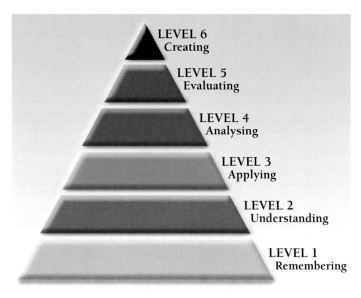

**BLOOM'S TAXONOMY:
6 LEVELS OF THINKING**

Bloom's Taxonomy is a tool widely used by educators for classifying learning objectives, and is based on the work of Benjamin Bloom.

Vocabulary

ant	bucket	door	hand	nut	sock
arm	button	drawer	hat	pen	spoon
apple	cake	dress	head	pencil	square
baby	camera	ear	heart	pig	star
bag	card	egg	horse	pin	stick
ball	cat	eye	hospital	plane	sun
bed	chain	face	house	plate	table
bee	cheese	farm	key	pot	tail
bell	chest	feather	knee	potato	thread
berry	chin	finger	leg	rat	thumb
bird	church	fish	lip	ring	toe
boat	circle	flag	lock	sail	tongue
bone	clock	floor	map	school	tooth
book	cloud	fly	monkey	scissors	tree
boot	coat	foot	moon	sheep	umbrella
bottle	comb	fork	mouth	ship	watch
box	cow	girl	nail	shirt	whistle
boy	cup	goat	neck	shoe	window
bridge	curtain	hair	net	skirt	wing
brush	dog	hammer	nose	snake	worm

NAME: _____

Boxed Picture Words Set#3

Read the words in the table. Use each word in the table once.
Write the letters in the box that match the shape of the word.
The boxes show tall and small letters.

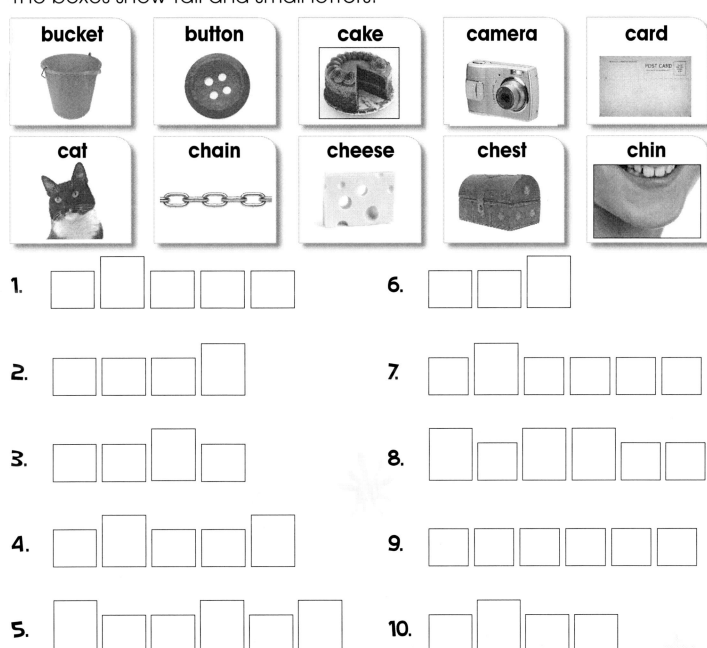

1.

2.

3.

4.

5.

6.

7.

8.

9.

10.

Write two sentences on the back using one picture word in each.

High-Frequency Picture Words CC1114

NAME: _____

Boxed Picture Words Set#4

Read the words in the table. Use each word in the table once.
Write the letters in the box that match the shape of the word.
The boxes show tall and small letters.

church 	circle 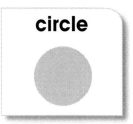	clock 	cloud 	coat 
comb 	cow 	cup 	curtain 	dog 

1. ☐☐☐☐

6. ☐☐☐

2. ☐☐☐☐☐☐

7. ☐☐☐☐☐

3. ☐☐☐☐☐☐

8. ☐☐☐☐☐☐☐

4. ☐☐☐☐

9. ☐☐☐

5. ☐☐☐☐☐

10. ☐☐☐

Write two sentences on the back using one picture word in each.

Boxed Picture Words Set#5

Read the words in the table. Use each word in the table once.
Write the letters in the box that match the shape of the word.
The boxes show tall and small letters.

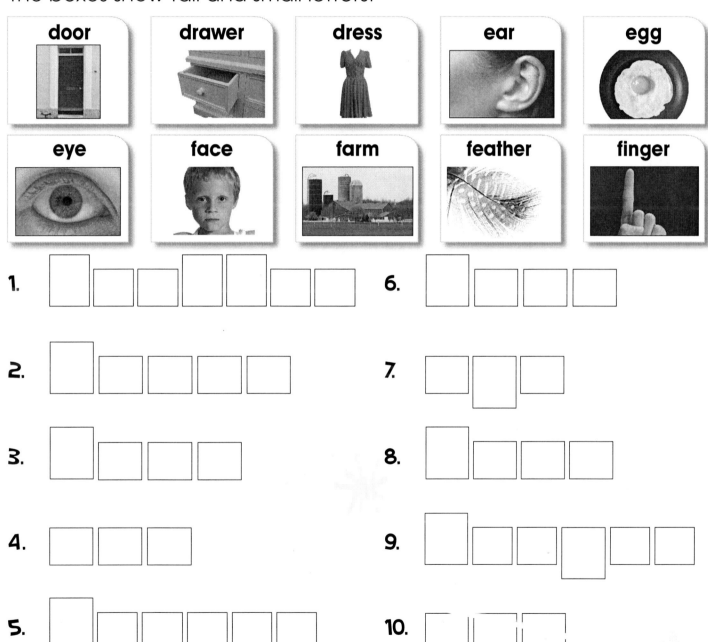

| door | drawer | dress | ear | egg |
| eye | face | farm | feather | finger |

1.

6.

2.

7.

3.

8.

4.

9.

5.

10.

Write two sentences on the back using one picture word in each.

Boxed Picture Words Set#6

Read the words in the table. Use each word in the table once.
Write the letters in the box that match the shape of the word.
The boxes show tall and small letters.

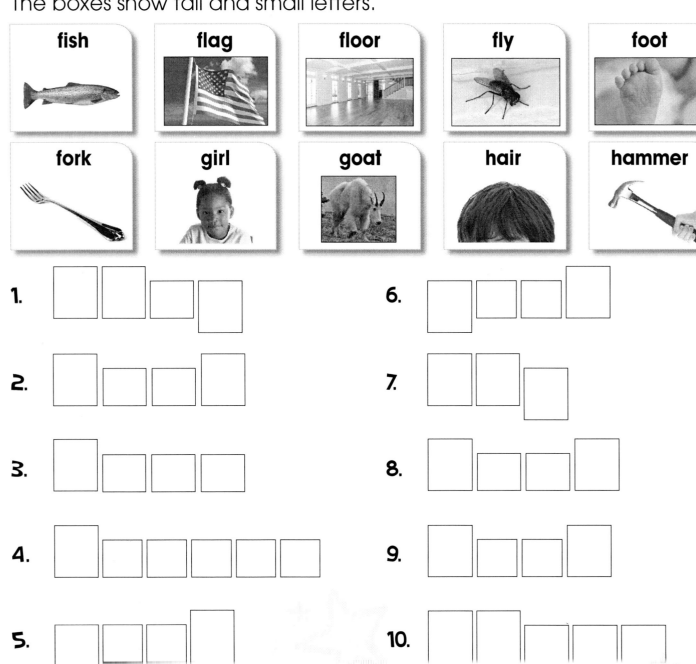

| fish | flag | floor | fly | foot |
| fork | girl | goat | hair | hammer |

1.

2.

3.

4.

5.

6.

7.

8.

9.

10.

Write two sentences on the back using one picture word in each.

NAME: _____

Boxed Picture Words Set#7

Read the words in the table. Use each word in the table once.
Write the letters in the box that match the shape of the word.
The boxes show tall and small letters.

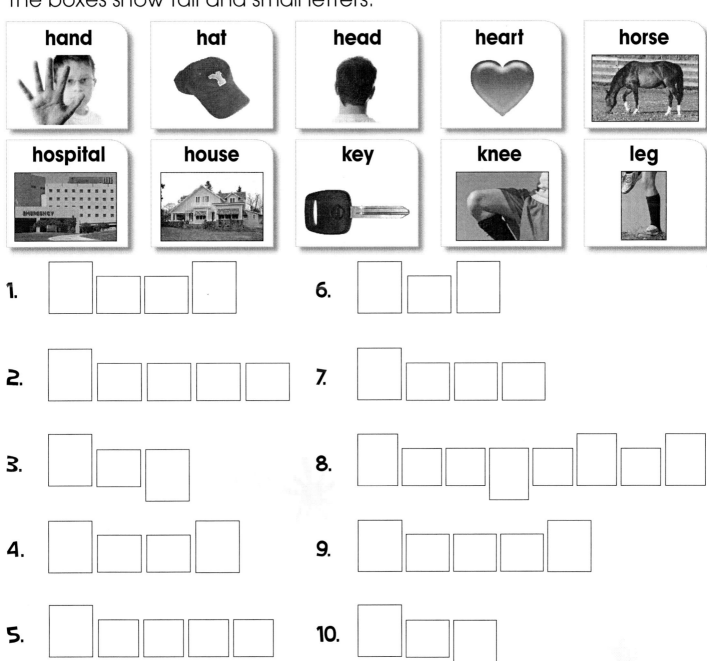

hand

hat

head

heart

horse

hospital

house

key

knee

leg

1.

2.

3.

4.

5.

6.

7.

8.

9.

10.

Write two sentences on the back using one picture word in each.

High-Frequency Picture Words CC1114

Boxed Picture Words Set#8

Read the words in the table. Use each word in the table once.
Write the letters in the box that match the shape of the word.
The boxes show tall and small letters.

lip	lock	map	monkey	moon

mouth	nail	neck	net	nose
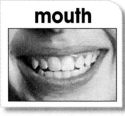		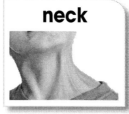	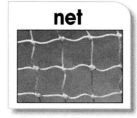	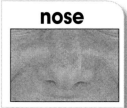

1.

2.

3.

4.

5.

6.

7.

8.

9.

10.

Write two sentences on the back using one picture word in each.

High-Frequency Picture Words CC1114

Working With Words

Boxed Picture Words Set#9

Read the words in the table. Use each word in the table once.
Write the letters in the box that match the shape of the word.
The boxes show tall and small letters.

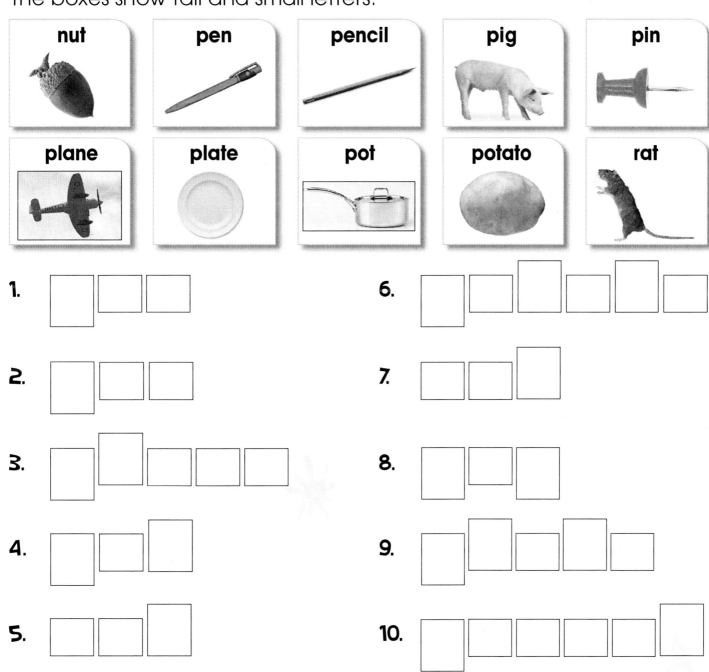

nut

pen

pencil

pig

pin

plane

plate

pot

potato

rat

1.

2.

3.

4.

5.

6.

7.

8.

9.

10.

Write two sentences on the back using one picture word in each.

High-Frequency Picture Words CC1114

NAME: _____

Boxed Picture Words Set#10

Read the words in the table. Use each word in the table once.
Write the letters in the box that match the shape of the word.
The boxes show tall and small letters.

ring	sail	school	scissors	sheep

ship	shirt	shoe	skirt	snake

1.

6.

2.

7.

3.

8.

4.

9.

5.

10.

Write two sentences on the back using one picture word in each.

18

Boxed Picture Words Set#11

Read the words in the table. Use each word in the table once.
Write the letters in the box that match the shape of the word.
The boxes show tall and small letters.

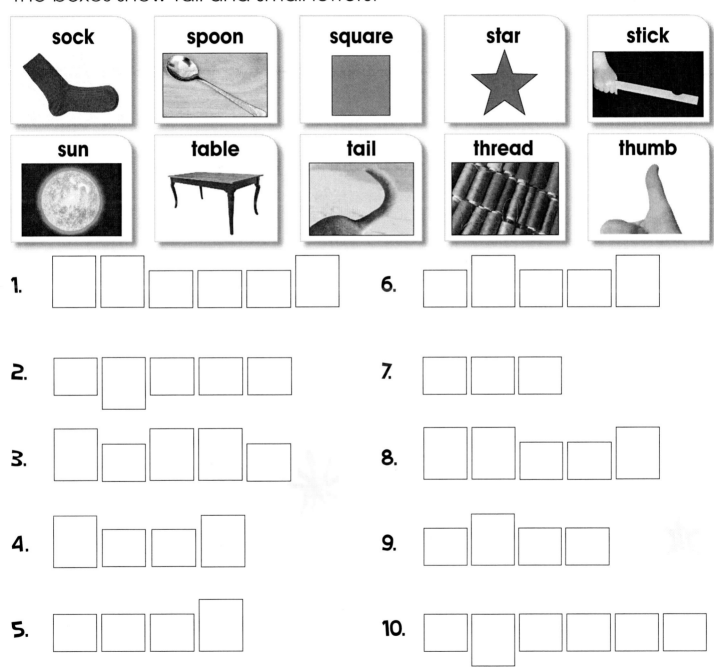

Write two sentences on the back using one picture word in each.

Boxed Picture Words Set#12

Read the words in the table. Use each word in the table once.
Write the letters in the box that match the shape of the word.
The boxes show tall and small letters.

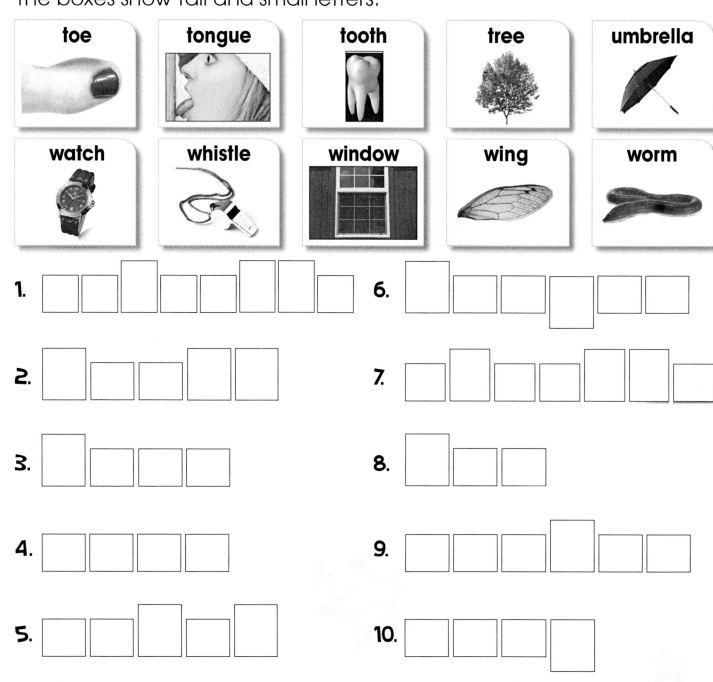

| toe | tongue | tooth | tree | umbrella |
| watch | whistle | window | wing | worm |

1. ▢▢▢▢▢▢▢   6. ▢▢▢▢▢▢

2. ▢▢▢▢▢   7. ▢▢▢▢▢▢

3. ▢▢▢   8. ▢▢▢

4. ▢▢▢▢   9. ▢▢▢▢▢▢

5. ▢▢▢▢▢   10. ▢▢▢▢

Write two sentences on the back using one picture word in each.

Picture Word Sentence Completion Set#2

Choose a word from the box to make the sentence complete. The boxes show tall and small letters. **The first one has been done for you.**

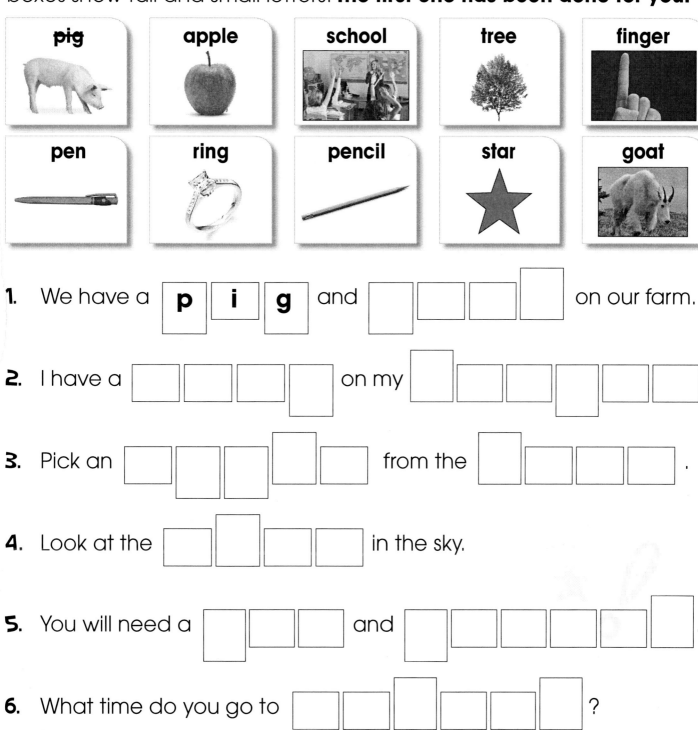

pig · **apple** · **school** · **tree** · **finger**

pen · **ring** · **pencil** · **star** · **goat**

1. We have a | p | i | g | and ☐☐☐☐ on our farm.

2. I have a ☐☐☐☐ on my ☐☐☐☐☐☐.

3. Pick an ☐☐☐☐☐ from the ☐☐☐☐.

4. Look at the ☐☐☐☐ in the sky.

5. You will need a ☐☐☐ and ☐☐☐☐☐☐.

6. What time do you go to ☐☐☐☐☐☐ ?

Picture Word Sentence Completion Set#3

Choose a word from the box to make the sentence complete. The boxes show tall and small letters. **The first one has been done for you.**

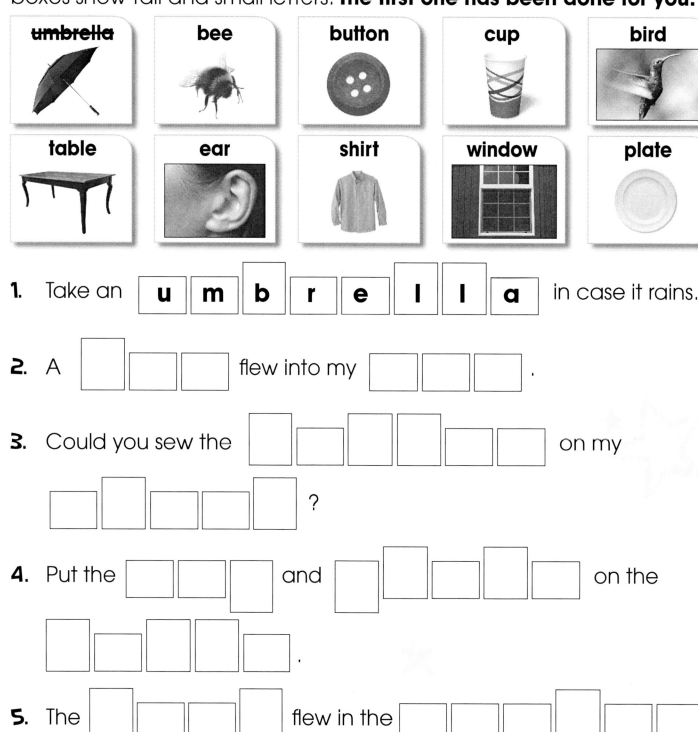

| ~~umbrella~~ | bee | button | cup | bird |

| table | ear | shirt | window | plate |

1. Take an `u` `m` `b` `r` `e` `l` `l` `a` in case it rains.

2. A ☐☐☐ flew into my ☐☐☐ .

3. Could you sew the ☐☐☐☐☐ on my ☐☐☐☐ ?

4. Put the ☐☐☐ and ☐☐☐☐☐ on the ☐☐☐☐☐ .

5. The ☐☐☐☐ flew in the ☐☐☐☐☐☐ .

Match and Print Words Set#1

Examine the word box. Select the boxes that match the shape of the word. Write a letter from the word in each box until the boxes are all filled. Then print the word on the lines. Draw a picture of the word in the last column.

dog   fly   fish   sail   bird   goat   rat   pig

Match and Print Words Set#2

Examine the word box. Select the boxes that match the shape of the word. Write a letter from the word in each box until the boxes are all filled. Then print the word on the lines. Draw a picture of the word in the last column.

head   comb   ring   brush   bed   apple   sun   nose   star

NAME: _____

Writing Task: Silly Sentences

Create silly sentences using the picture words. Write three sentences and illustrate them.

For example: The orange <u>goat</u> ate a purple <u>boot</u>.

1. _____

_____

2. _____

_____

3. _____

_____

 Flash Cards

ant	arm	apple
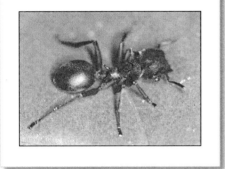		

baby	bag	ball
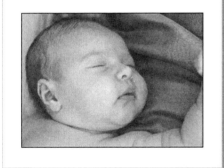		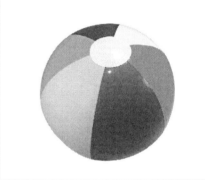

bed	bee	bell

berry

bird

boat

bone

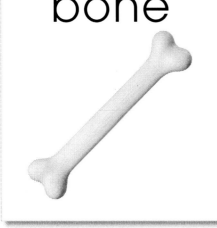

book

boot

bottle

box

boy

 **NAME:** _____

bridge

brush

bucket

button

cake

camera

card

cat

chain

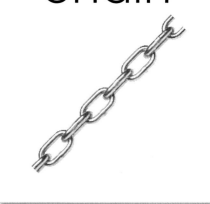

cheese

chest

chin

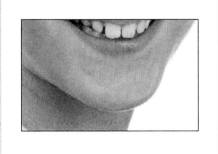

church

circle

clock

cloud

coat

comb

High-Frequency Picture Words CC1114

cow

cup

curtain

dog

door

drawer

dress

ear

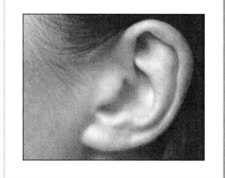

egg

eye
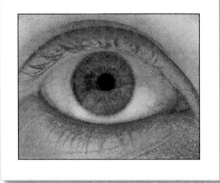

face

farm

feather

finger

fish

flag

floor

fly

High-Frequency Picture Words CC1114

foot

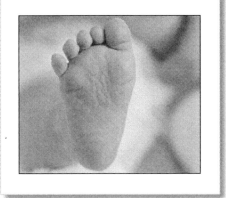

fork

girl

goat

hair

hammer

hand

hat

head

heart

horse

hospital

house

key

knee
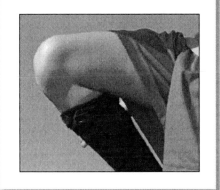

leg

lip
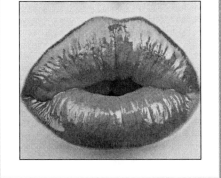

lock

 Flash Cards

map

monkey

moon

mouth

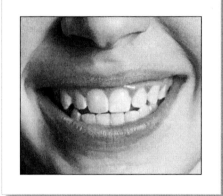

nail

neck

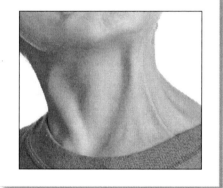

net

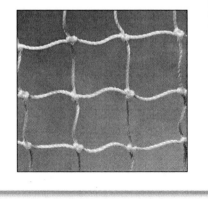

nose

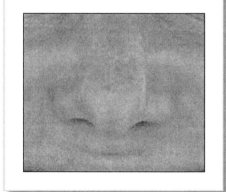

nut

pen

pencil

pig

pin

plane

plate

pot

potato

rat

 NAME: _____

ring

sail

school

scissors

sheep

ship

shirt

shoe

skirt

High-Frequency Picture Words CC1114

snake 	sock 	spoon 
square 	star 	stick 
sun 	table 	tail 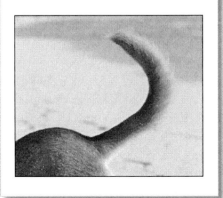

High-Frequency Picture Words CC1114

Crossword Puzzle

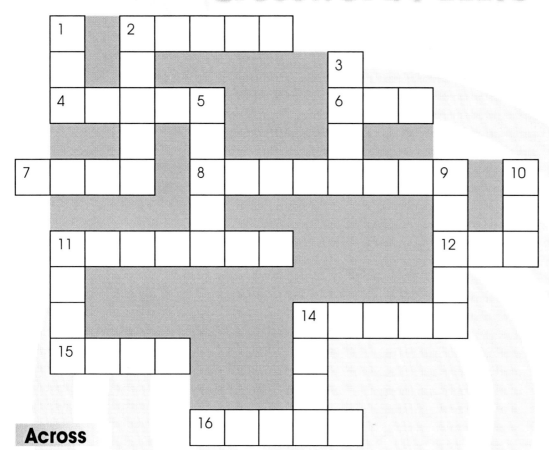

Word List

ant
apple
brush
dog
eyes
face
feather
heart
house
knee
pig
rat
skirt
snake
star
thumb
tree
umbrella

Across

2. the shape of love
4. you have four fingers and one _____
6. a rodent with a long tail
7. rhymes with "bee"
8. it keeps the rain off your head
11. a bird has many of these
12. this animal says, "oink"
14. crawls on the ground and says, "s.s.s."
15. you see with your _____
16. worn like pants with a shirt

Down

1. small insect that lives in colonies
2. where you live
3. where wood comes from
5. you comb or _____ your hair
9. a red or green fruit that makes juice
10. a furry pet
11. where your eyes, ears, nose and mouth are
14. shines in the dark sky

MY NAME: _____

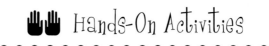

Word Search

Find all of the words in the Word Search. Words are written horizontally, vertically, diagonally, and some are even written backwards.

apple	card	drawer	key	potato	spoon
baby	coat	feather	lock	rat	table
boot	chest	hammer	monkey	sheep	thread
box	curtain	horse	pencil	shirt	umbrella
					whistle

r	e	s	r	o	h	f	r	d	o	o	t	a	t	o	p
a	r	p	l	c	a	r	d	n	c	s	q	a	s	i	t
c	v	a	k	h	i	r	a	d	u	s	r	a	d	t	w
a	p	p	l	e	o	e	d	u	h	h	p	i	r	r	c
j	e	b	e	s	t	f	m	m	s	e	o	b	a	b	y
a	n	l	p	t	d	t	a	b	l	e	s	s	w	q	a
m	c	a	m	y	i	n	r	r	o	p	o	e	e	a	b
r	i	c	w	e	d	h	f	e	a	t	h	e	r	d	n
o	l	o	c	k	c	t	a	l	l	y	a	u	b	t	i
r	a	t	w	h	n	n	z	l	b	l	m	n	b	y	a
s	t	h	e	b	o	b	j	a	u	o	m	t	e	w	t
g	u	r	y	t	o	l	u	e	n	q	e	r	e	i	r
b	e	e	c	o	p	x	m	k	d	l	r	i	v	l	u
c	o	a	t	a	s	o	e	w	i	k	w	h	l	l	c
e	t	d	t	t	d	y	o	l	e	l	t	s	i	h	w

High-Frequency Picture Words CC1114

Comprehension Quiz

25

Circle the answer that is correct.

1. Which word is not a picture word?

   a) it   **b)** cat   **c)** pot   **1**

2. Which word will not fit?

   a) key   **b)** bee   **c)** bag   **1**

3. Which word cannot be eaten?

   a) cheese   **b)** apple   **c)** watch   **1**

4. Which word is not an animal?

   a) toe   **b)** cow   **c)** pig   **1**

5. Which sentence has two picture words in it?

   a) The cat and dog ran.

   b) I have a plane.

   c) She went to school.   **1**

Circle **T** if the statement is TRUE **or** **F** if it is FALSE.   **5**

T F   **a)** "Tree" is a picture word.

T F   **b)** "The, at, in" are picture words.

T F   **c)** "Hand, finger, thumb" are body part picture words.

T F   **d)** "Green, yellow, orange" are picture words.

T F   **e)** "Bee" and "ball" rhyme.

SUBTOTAL: /10

Comprehension Quiz

Answer the questions in complete sentences.

1. What is a picture word? Give an example.

_____

_____

_____

2. List six picture words:

_____   _____   _____

_____   _____   _____

3. Draw a line connecting the picture and matching word.

a)    **pencil**

b) 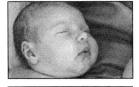   **baby**

c)    **worm**

d)    **sun**

e)    **cake**

SUBTOTAL: /15

1. arm
2. berry
3. bag
4. apple
5. baby
6. ant
7. ball
8. bell
9. bed
10. bee

Answers will vary.

⑨

---

1. bone
2. bottle
3. bridge
4. bird
5. brush
6. box
7. book
8. boat
9. boy
10. boot

Answers will vary.

⑩

---

1. chain
2. card
3. cake
4. chest
5. bucket
6. cat
7. cheese
8. button
9. camera
10. chin

Answers will vary.

⑪

---

1. comb
2. circle
3. church
4. coat
5. cloud
6. cow
7. clock
8. curtain
9. dog
10. cup

Answers will vary.

⑫

---

1. feather
2. dress
3. door
4. ear
5. drawer
6. farm
7. eye
8. face
9. finger
10. egg

Answers will vary.

⑬

---

1. flag
2. fork
3. hair
4. hammer
5. girl
6. goat
7. fly
8. foot
9. fish
10. floor

Answers will vary.

⑭

NAME: _____

Boxed Picture Words Set#2

Read the words in the table. Use each word in the table once.
Write the letters in the box that match the shape of the word.
The boxes show tall and small letters.

bird 	boat 	bone 	book 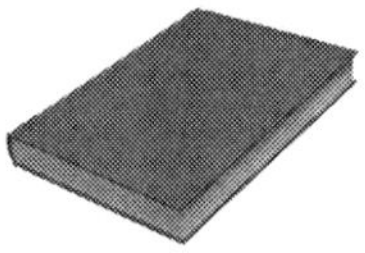	boot 

bottle 	box 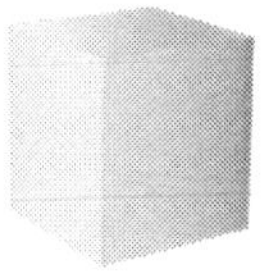	boy 	bridge 	brush 

1. ☐☐☐☐

2. ☐☐☐☐☐☐

3. ☐☐☐☐☐

4. ☐☐☐☐

5. ☐☐☐☐☐

6. ☐☐☐

7. ☐☐☐☐

8. ☐☐☐

9. ☐☐☐

10. ☐☐☐☐

Write two sentences on the back using one picture word in each.

NAME: _____

 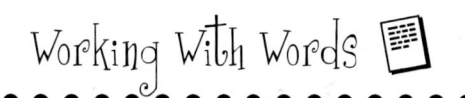

Boxed Picture Words Set#1

Read the words in the table. Use each word in the table once.
Write the letters in the box that match the shape of the word.
The boxes show tall and small letters.

ant 	arm 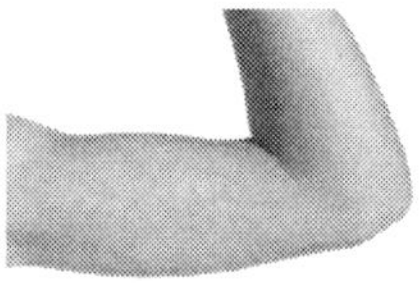	apple 	baby 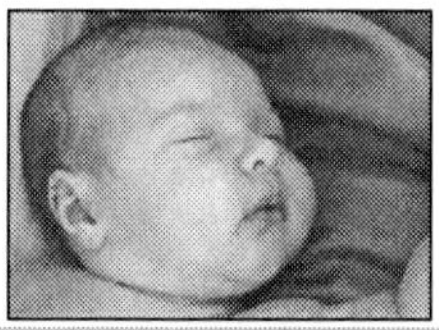	bag 
ball 	bed 	bee 	bell 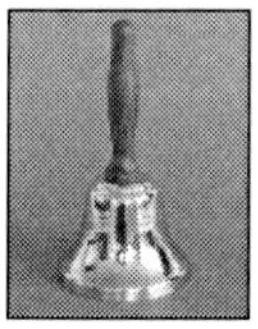	berry 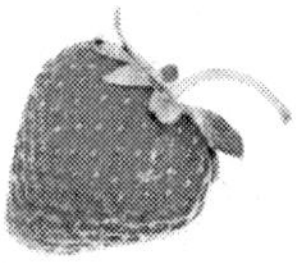

1. ☐☐☐

6. ☐☐☐

2. ☐☐☐☐☐

7. ☐☐☐☐

3. ☐☐☐

8. ☐☐☐☐

4. ☐☐☐☐☐

9. ☐☐☐

5. ☐☐☐☐

10. ☐☐☐

Write two sentences on the back using one picture word in each.

1. head	1. lock	1. pen	1. sheep	1. thread	1. umbrella
2. horse	2. nose	2. pin	2. shirt	2. spoon	2. tooth
3. leg	3. neck	3. plane	3. skirt	3. table	3. tree
4. hand	4. map	4. pot	4. shoe	4. tail	4. worm
5. house	5. lip	5. nut	5. sail	5. sock	5. watch
6. hat	6. net	6. potato	6. ship	6. stick	6. tongue
7. knee	7. nail	7. rat	7. ring	7. sun	7. whistle
8. hospital	8. mouth	8. pig	8. snake	8. thumb	8. toe
9. heart	9. moon	9. plate	9. scissors	9. star	9. window
10. key	10. monkey	10. pencil	10. school	10. square	10. wing
Answers will vary.	Answers will vary.	Answers will vary.	Answers will vary.	Answers will vary.	Answers will vary.
15	16	17	18	19	20

EZ✔

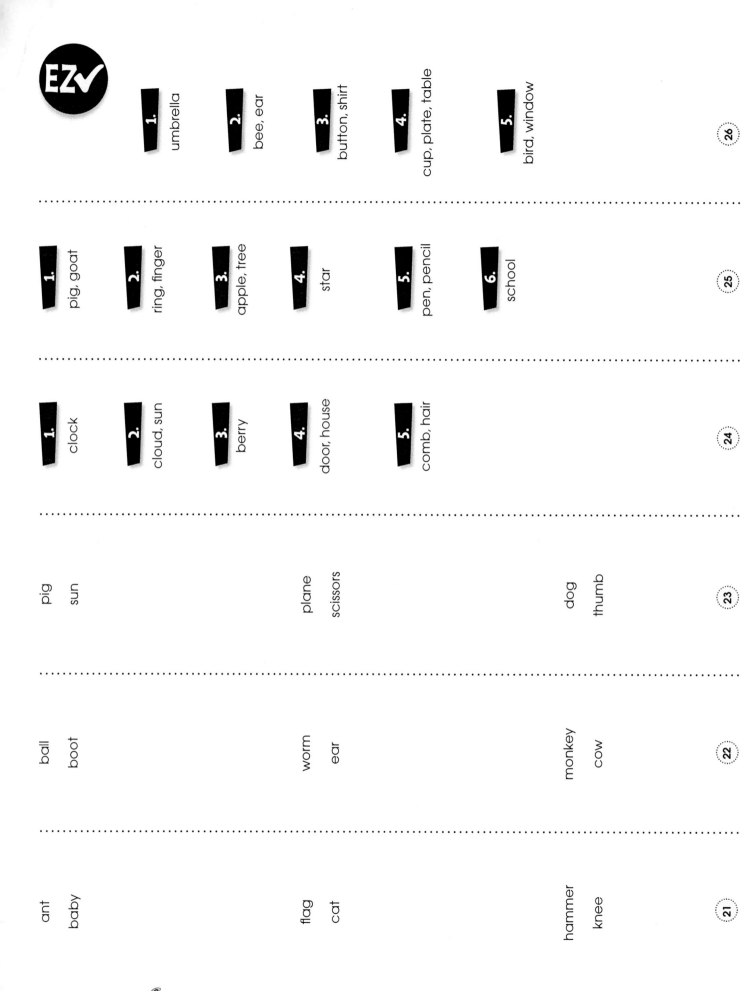

1. umbrella
2. bee, ear
3. button, shirt
4. cup, plate, table
5. bird, window

26

1. pig, goat
2. ring, finger
3. apple, tree
4. star
5. pen, pencil
6. school

25

1. clock
2. cloud, sun
3. berry
4. door, house
5. comb, hair

24

pig
sun

plane
scissors

dog
thumb

23

ball
boot

worm
ear

monkey
cow

22

ant
baby

flag
cat

hammer
knee

21

shirt

boot

coat

shoe

dress

sock

---

berry

cake

nut

potato

apple

egg

---

thumb

finger

hand

ear

arm

eye

---

1. face

2. fork

3. pen

4. spoon

5. bell

---

1. comb

2. brush

3. sun

4. head

5. bed

---

1. rat

2. fish

3. bird

4. dog

5. fly

Answers will vary.

1. A picture word is a common noun – people, places or things. Common nouns are vocabulary words found frequently in print. Picture words are words that we should know to help us read and understand our environment. (2 points for an explanation) Example: brown, thumb, shirt, etc. (1 point for an example)

2. Any six sight words – 1 point each

3.
a) sun
b) baby
c) cake
d) pencil
e) worm

49

1. a)

2. b)

3. c)

4. a)

5. a)

a) T
b) F
c) T
d) F
e) F

48

Word Search Answers

47

Across
2. heart
4. thumb
6. rat
7. knee
8. umbrella
11. feather
12. pig
14. snake
15. eyes
16. skirt

Down
1. ant
2. house
3. tree
5. brush
9. apple
10. dog
11. face
14. star

46

Answers will vary.

Sounds the Same

• •

In the column on the left, record five picture words. Say the word. Draw a picture of the word. Think of other words that sound like the picture word. Write three words in the right column that rhyme with the picture word in the left column.

Picture Word	Picture	Rhyming Words
_____		_____ _____ _____
_____		_____ _____ _____
_____		_____ _____ _____
_____		_____ _____ _____
_____		_____ _____ _____

Write the Room

● ● ● ● ● ● ● ● ● ● ● ● ● ● ● ● ● ● ●

Look around the classroom for picture words. Record five of them on the lines below. Draw a picture to illustrate each word.

Word	Picture
1. _____	
2. _____	
3. _____	
4. _____	
5. _____	

Use the Clues

● ● ● ● ● ● ● ● ● ● ● ● ● ● ● ● ● ●

Read each clue. Think of which picture word matches the clue.
Write the word on the line in the guess column. Read the next clue
and make another guess.

Clue	Guess
1. This word has _____ letters.	_____
2. This word has _____ syllables.	_____
3. This word has _____ sounds.	_____
4. This word rhymes with _____.	_____
5. This word looks like this:	_____

Picture Word Chart

1. Choose a picture word. Think of three other words that are connected to the picture word at the top. Draw a quick sketch of each picture word.

2. How are these words related?

Predict the Hidden Word

● ● ● ● ● ● ● ● ● ● ● ● ● ● ● ● ● ●

Mary's Farm

On Mary's farm we get to play with lots of animals.

She has a pig. He likes to lie in the mud. She also has a

cow who gives her milk. She makes cheese from the milk. She

also has a goat. They live outside, in the barn.

We like to pet the dog and the cat.   They live with her in the

house. She takes them for rides on the tractor.

Mary takes us for rides on her horse. We take the horse

for long rides on the trail.

Add the Blend or Digraph

Add fl, pl, sh or ch to make picture words. Write the letters on the lines to make words. Draw a picture of the word in the box.

___ ___ eep	___ ___ ate	___ ___ ip
___ ___ est	___ ___ ag	___ ___ ain
___ ___ irt	___ ___ ane	___ ___ y
___ ___ eese	___ ___ oe	___ ___ ain

- **RSIT.K.4** With prompting and support, ask and answer questions about unknown words in a text.
- **RSIT.K.7** With prompting and support, describe the relationship between illustrations and the text in which they appear.
- **RSIT.K.10** Actively engage in group reading activities with purpose and understanding.
- **RSIT.1.4** Ask and answer questions to help determine or clarify the meaning of words and phrases in a text.
- **RSIT.1.5** Know and use various text features to locate key facts or information in a text.
- **RSIT.1.6** Distinguish between information provided by pictures or other illustrations and information provided by the words in a text.
- **RSIT.1.7** Use the illustrations and details in a text to describe its key ideas.
- **RSIT.1.10** With prompting and support, read informational texts appropriately complex for grade 1.
- **RSFS.K.1** Demonstrate understanding of the organization and basic features of print. **A)** Follow words from left to right, top to bottom, and page by page. **B)** Recognize that spoken words are represented in written language by specific sequences of letters. **C)** Understand that words are separated by spaces in print. **D)** Recognize and name all upper- and lowercase letters of the alphabet.
- **RSFS.K.2** Demonstrate understanding of spoken words, syllables, and sounds. **A)** Recognize and produce rhyming words. **B)** Count, pronounce, blend, and segment syllables in spoken words. **C)** Blend and segment onsets and rimes of single-syllable spoken words. **D)** Isolate and pronounce the initial, medial vowel, and final sounds in three-phoneme words. **E)** Add or substitute individual sounds in simple, one-syllable words to make new words.
- **RSFS.K.3** Know and apply grade-level phonics and word analysis skills in decoding words. **A)** Demonstrate basic knowledge of one-to-one letter-sound correspondences by producing the primary sound or many of the most frequent sounds for each consonant. **B)** Associate the long and short sounds with common spellings for the five major vowels. **C)** Read common high-frequency words by sight. **D)** Distinguish between similarly spelled words by identifying the sounds of the letters that differ.
- **RSFS.1.2** Demonstrate understanding of spoken words, syllables, and sounds. **A)** Distinguish long from short vowel sounds in spoken single-syllable words. **B)** Orally produce single-syllable words by blending sounds, including consonant blends. **C)** Isolate and pronounce initial, medial vowel, and final sounds in spoken single-syllable words. **D)** Segment spoken single-syllable words into their complete sequence of individual sounds.
- **RSFS.1.3** Know and apply grade-level phonics and word analysis skills in decoding words. **A)** Know the spelling-sound correspondences for common consonant digraphs. **B)** Decode regularly spelled one-syllable words. **C)** Know final -e and common vowel team conventions for representing long vowel sounds. **D)** Use knowledge that every syllable must have a vowel sound to determine the number of syllables in a printed word. **E)** Decode two-syllable words following basic patterns by breaking the words into syllables. **F)** Read words with inflectional endings. **G)** Recognize and read grade-appropriate irregularly spelled words.
- **SLS.K.1** Participate in collaborative conversations with diverse partners about *kindergarten topics and texts* with peers and adults in small and larger groups. **A)** Follow agreed-upon rules for discussions. **B)** Continue a conversation through multiple exchanges.
- **SLS.K.3** Ask and answer questions in order to seek help, get information, or clarify something that is not understood.
- **SLS.K.5** Add drawings or other visual displays to descriptions as desired to provide additional detail.
- **SLS.K.6** Speak audibly and express thoughts, feelings, and ideas clearly.
- **SLS.1.1** Participate in collaborative conversations with diverse partners about *grade 1 topics and texts* with peers and adults in small and larger groups. **A)** Follow agreed-upon rules for discussions. **B)** Build on others' talk in conversations by responding to the comments of others through multiple exchanges. **C)** Ask questions to clear up any confusion about the topics and texts under discussion.
- **SLS.1.3** Ask and answer questions about what a speaker says in order to gather additional information or clarify something that is not understood.
- **SLS.1.4** Describe people, places, things, and events with relevant details, expressing ideas and feelings clearly.
- **SLS.1.5** Add drawings or other visual displays to descriptions when appropriate to clarify ideas, thoughts, and feelings.
- **SLS.1.6** Produce complete sentences when appropriate to task and situation.
- **LS.K.1** Demonstrate command of the conventions of standard English grammar and usage when writing or speaking. **A)** Print many upper- and lowercase letters. **B)** Use frequently occurring nouns and verbs. **C)** Form regular plural nouns orally by adding /s/ or /es/. **D)** Understand and use question words. **E)** Use the most frequently occurring prepositions. **F)** Produce and expand complete sentences in shared language activities.
- **LS.K.2** Demonstrate command of the conventions of standard English capitalization, punctuation, and spelling when writing. **A)** Capitalize the first word in a sentence and the pronoun. **B)** Recognize and name end punctuation. **C)** Write a letter or letters for most consonant and short-vowel sounds. **D)** Spell simple words phonetically, drawing on knowledge of sound-letter relationships.
- **LS.K.4** Determine or clarify the meaning of unknown and multiple-meaning words and phrases based on *kindergarten reading and content.* **A)** Identify new meanings for familiar words and apply them accurately. **B)** Use the most frequently occurring inflections and affixes as a clue to the meaning of an unknown word.
- **LS.K.5** With guidance and support from adults, explore word relationships and nuances in word meanings. **A)** Sort common objects into categories to gain a sense of the concepts the categories represent. **B)** Demonstrate understanding of frequently occurring verbs and adjectives by relating them to their opposites. **C)** Identify real-life connections between words and their use. **D)** Distinguish shades of meaning among verbs describing the same general action by acting out the meanings.
- **LS.K.6** Use words and phrases acquired through conversations, reading and being read to, and responding to texts.
- **LS.1.1** Demonstrate command of the conventions of standard English grammar and usage when writing or speaking. **A)** Print all upper- and lowercase letters. **B)** Use common, proper, and possessive nouns. **C)** Use singular and plural nouns with matching verbs in basic sentences. **D)** Use personal, possessive, and indefinite pronouns. **E)** Use verbs to convey a sense of past, present, and future. **F)** Use frequently occurring adjectives. **G)** Use frequently occurring conjunctions. **H)** Use determiners. **I)** Use frequently occurring prepositions. **J)** Produce and expand complete simple and compound declarative, interrogative, imperative, and exclamatory sentences in response to prompts.
- **LS.1.2** Demonstrate command of the conventions of standard English capitalization, punctuation, and spelling when writing. **A)** Capitalize dates and names of people. **B)** Use end punctuation for sentences. **C)** Use commas in dates and to separate single words in a series. **D)** Use conventional spelling for words with common spelling patterns and for frequently occurring irregular words. **E)** Spell untaught words phonetically, drawing on phonemic awareness and spelling conventions.
- **LS.1.4** Determine or clarify the meaning of unknown and multiple-meaning words and phrases based on *grade 1 reading and content*, choosing flexibly from an array of strategies. **A)** Use sentence-level context as a clue to the meaning of a word or phrase. **B)** Use frequently occurring affixes as a clue to the meaning of a word. **C)** Identify frequently occurring root words and their inflectional forms.
- **LS.1.5** With guidance and support from adults, demonstrate understanding of word relationships and nuances in word meanings. **A)** Sort words into categories to gain a sense of the concepts the categories represent. **B)** Define words by category and by one or more key attributes. **C)** Identify real-life connections between words and their use. **D)** Distinguish shades of meaning among verbs differing in manner and adjectives differing in intensity by defining or choosing them or by acting out the meanings.
- **LS.1.6** Use words and phrases acquired through conversations, reading and being read to, and responding to texts, including using frequently occurring conjunctions to signal simple relationships.

Publication Listing

• • • • • • • • • • • • • • • • •

Ask Your Dealer About Our Complete Line

SOCIAL STUDIES - Software

ITEM #	TITLE
	MAPPING SKILLS SERIES
CC7770	Grades PK-2 Mapping Skills with Google Earth
CC7771	Grades 3-5 Mapping Skills with Google Earth
CC7772	Grades 6-8 Mapping Skills with Google Earth
CC7773	Grades PK-8 Mapping Skills with Google Earth Big Box

SOCIAL STUDIES - Books

ITEM #	TITLE
	MAPPING SKILLS SERIES
CC5786	Grades PK-2 Mapping Skills with Google Earth
CC5787	Grades 3-5 Mapping Skills with Google Earth
CC5788	Grades 6-8 Mapping Skills with Google Earth
CC5789	Grades PK-8 Mapping Skills with Google Earth Big Book
	NORTH AMERICAN GOVERNMENTS SERIES
CC5757	American Government
CC5758	Canadian Government
CC5759	Mexican Government
CC5760	Governments of North America Big Book
	WORLD GOVERNMENTS SERIES
CC5761	World Political Leaders
CC5762	World Electoral Processes
CC5763	Capitalism vs. Communism
CC5777	World Politics Big Book
	WORLD CONFLICT SERIES
CC5511	American Revolutionary War
CC5500	American Civil War
CC5512	American Wars Big Book
CC5501	World War I
CC5502	World War II
CC5503	World Wars I & II Big Book
CC5505	Korean War
CC5506	Vietnam War
CC5507	Korean & Vietnam Wars Big Book
CC5508	Persian Gulf War (1990-1991)
CC5509	Iraq War (2003-2010)
CC5510	Gulf Wars Big Book
	WORLD CONTINENTS SERIES
CC5750	North America
CC5751	South America
CC5768	The Americas Big Book
CC5752	Europe
CC5753	Africa
CC5754	Asia
CC5755	Australia
CC5756	Antarctica
	WORLD CONNECTIONS SERIES
CC5782	Culture, Society & Globalization
CC5783	Economy & Globalization
CC5784	Technology & Globalization
CC5785	Globalization Big Book

REGULAR & REMEDIAL EDUCATION

• • • • • • • • • • • • • • • •

Reading Level 3-4 Grades 5-8

ENVIRONMENTAL STUDIES - Software

ITEM #	TITLE
	CLIMATE CHANGE SERIES
CC7747	Global Warming: Causes Grades 3-8
CC7748	Global Warming: Effects Grades 3-8
CC7749	Global Warming: Reduction Grades 3-8
CC7750	Global Warming Big Box Grades 3-8

ENVIRONMENTAL STUDIES - Books

ITEM #	TITLE
	MANAGING OUR WASTE SERIES
CC5764	Waste: At the Source
CC5765	Prevention, Recycling & Conservation
CC5766	Waste: The Global View
CC5767	Waste Management Big Book
	CLIMATE CHANGE SERIES
CC5769	Global Warming: Causes
CC5770	Global Warming: Effects
CC5771	Global Warming: Reduction
CC5772	Global Warming Big Book
	GLOBAL WATER SERIES
CC5773	Conservation: Fresh Water Resources
CC5774	Conservation: Ocean Water Resources
CC5775	Conservation: Waterway Habitat Resources
CC5776	Water Conservation Big Book
	CARBON FOOTPRINT SERIES
CC5778	Reducing Your Own Carbon Footprint
CC5779	Reducing Your School's Carbon Footprint
CC5780	Reducing Your Community's Carbon Footprint
CC5781	Carbon Footprint Big Book

SCIENCE - Software

ITEM #	TITLE
	SPACE AND BEYOND SERIES
CC7557	Solar System Grades 5-8
CC7558	Galaxies & the Universe Grades 5-8
CC7559	Space Travel & Technology Grades 5-8
CC7560	Space Big Box Grades 5-8
	HUMAN BODY SERIES
CC7549	Cells, Skeletal & Muscular Systems Grades 5-8
CC7550	Senses, Nervous & Respiratory Systems Grades 5-8
CC7551	Circulatory, Digestive & Reproductive Systems Grades 5-8
CC7552	Human Body Big Box Grades 5-8
	FORCE, MOTION & SIMPLE MACHINES SERIES
CC7553	Force Grades 3-8
CC7554	Motion Grades 3-8
CC7555	Simple Machines Grades 3-8
CC7556	Force, Motion & Simple Machines Big Box Grades 3-8

SCIENCE - Books

ITEM #	TITLE
	ECOLOGY & THE ENVIRONMENT SERIES
CC4500	Ecosystems
CC4501	Classification & Adaptation
CC4502	Cells
CC4503	Ecology & The Environment Big Book
	MATTER & ENERGY SERIES
CC4504	Properties of Matter
CC4505	Atoms, Molecules & Elements
CC4506	Energy
CC4507	The Nature of Matter Big Book
	FORCE & MOTION SERIES
CC4508	Force
CC4509	Motion
CC4510	Simple Machines
CC4511	Force, Motion & Simple Machines Big Book
	SPACE & BEYOND SERIES
CC4512	Solar System
CC4513	Galaxies & The Universe
CC4514	Travel & Technology
CC4515	Space Big Book
	HUMAN BODY SERIES
CC4516	Cells, Skeletal & Muscular Systems
CC4517	Senses, Nervous & Respiratory Systems
CC4518	Circulatory, Digestive & Reproductive Systems
CC4519	Human Body Big Book

VISIT:

www.CLASSROOM COMPLETE PRESS.com

To view sample pages from each book

LITERATURE KITS™ - Books

ITEM #	TITLE
	GRADES 1-2
CC2100	Curious George (H. A. Rey)
CC2101	Paper Bag Princess (Robert N. Munsch)
CC2102	Stone Soup (Marcia Brown)
CC2103	The Very Hungry Caterpillar (Eric Carle)
CC2104	Where the Wild Things Are (Maurice Sendak)
	GRADES 3-4
CC2300	Babe: The Gallant Pig (Dick King-Smith)
CC2301	Because of Winn-Dixie (Kate DiCamillo)
CC2302	The Tale of Despereaux (Kate DiCamillo)
CC2303	James and the Giant Peach (Roald Dahl)
CC2304	Ramona Quimby, Age 8 (Beverly Cleary)
CC2305	The Mouse and the Motorcycle (Beverly Cleary)
CC2306	Charlotte's Web (E.B. White)
CC2307	Owls in the Family (Farley Mowat)
CC2308	Sarah, Plain and Tall (Patricia MacLachlan)
CC2309	Matilda (Roald Dahl)
CC2310	Charlie & The Chocolate Factory (Roald Dahl)
CC2311	Frindle (Andrew Clements)
CC2312	M.C. Higgins, the Great (Virginia Hamilton)
CC2313	The Family Under The Bridge (N.S. Carlson)
CC2314	The Hundred Penny Box (Sharon Mathis)
CC2315	Cricket in Times Square (George Selden)
CC2316	Fantastic Mr Fox (Roald Dahl)
CC2317	The Hundred Dresses (Eleanor Estes)
	GRADES 5-6
CC2500	Black Beauty (Anna Sewell)
CC2501	Bridge to Terabithia (Katherine Paterson)
CC2502	Bud, Not Buddy (Christopher Paul Curtis)
CC2503	The Egypt Game (Zilpha Keatley Snyder)
CC2504	The Great Gilly Hopkins (Katherine Paterson)
CC2505	Holes (Louis Sachar)
CC2506	Number the Stars (Lois Lowry)
CC2507	The Sign of the Beaver (E.G. Speare)
CC2508	The Whipping Boy (Sid Fleischman)
CC2509	Island of the Blue Dolphins (Scott O'Dell)
CC2510	Underground to Canada (Barbara Smucker)
CC2511	Loser (Jerry Spinelli)
CC2512	The Higher Power of Lucky (Susan Patron)
CC2513	Kira-Kira (Cynthia Kadohata)
CC2514	Dear Mr. Henshaw (Beverly Cleary)
CC2515	The Summer of the Swans (Betsy Byars)
CC2516	Shiloh (Phyllis Reynolds Naylor)
CC2517	A Single Shard (Linda Sue Park)
CC2518	Hoot (Carl Hiaasen)
CC2519	Hatchet (Gary Paulsen)
CC2520	The Giver (Lois Lowry)
CC2521	The Graveyard Book (Neil Gaiman)
CC2522	The View From Saturday (E.L. Konigsburg)
CC2523	Hattie Big Sky (Kirby Larson)
CC2524	When You Reach Me (Rebecca Stead)
CC2525	Criss Cross (Lynne Rae Perkins)
CC2526	A Year Down Yonder (Richard Peck)
CC2527	Maniac Magee (Jerry Spinelli)

LITERATURE KITS™ - Books

ITEM #	TITLE
CC2528	From the Mixed-Up Files of Mrs. Basil E. Frankweiler (E.L. Konigsburg)
CC2529	Sing Down the Moon (Scott O'Dell)
	GRADES 7-8
CC2700	Cheaper by the Dozen (Frank B. Gilbreth)
CC2701	The Miracle Worker (William Gibson)
CC2702	The Red Pony (John Steinbeck)
CC2703	Treasure Island (Robert Louis Stevenson)
CC2704	Romeo & Juliet (William Shakespeare)
CC2705	Crispin: The Cross of Lead (Avi)
CC2707	The Boy in the Striped Pajamas (John Boyne)
CC2708	The Westing Game (Ellen Raskin)
	GRADES 9-12
CC2001	To Kill A Mockingbird (Harper Lee)
CC2002	Angela's Ashes (Frank McCourt)
CC2003	The Grapes of Wrath (John Steinbeck)
CC2004	The Good Earth (Pearl S. Buck)
CC2005	The Road (Cormac McCarthy)
CC2006	The Old Man and the Sea (Ernest Hemingway)
CC2007	Lord of the Flies (William Golding)
CC2008	The Color Purple (Alice Walker)
CC2009	The Outsiders (S.E. Hinton)
CC2010	Hamlet (William Shakespeare)
CC2012	The Adventures of Huckleberry Finn (Mark Twain)
CC2013	Macbeth (William Shakespeare)

LANGUAGE ARTS - Software

ITEM #	TITLE
CC7112	**Word Families - Short Vowels Grades PK-2**
CC7113	**Word Families - Long Vowels Grades PK-2**
CC7114	**Word Families - Vowels Big Box Grades PK-2**
CC7100	**High Frequency Sight Words Grades PK-2**
CC7101	**High Frequency Picture Words Grades PK-2**
CC7102	**Sight & Picture Words Big Box Grades PK-2**
CC7104	**How to Write a Paragraph Grades 3-8**
CC7105	**How to Write a Book Report Grades 3-8**
CC7106	**How to Write an Essay Grades 3-8**
CC7107	**Master Writing Big Box Grades 3-8**
CC7108	**Reading Comprehension Grades 5-8**
CC7109	**Literary Devices Grades 5-8**
CC7110	**Critical Thinking Grades 5-8**
CC7111	**Master Reading Big Box Grades 5-8**

LANGUAGE ARTS - Books

ITEM #	TITLE
CC1110	**Word Families - Short Vowels Grades K-1**
CC1111	**Word Families - Long Vowels Grades K-1**
CC1112	**Word Families - Vowels Big Book Grades K-1**
CC1113	**High Frequency Sight Words Grades K-1**
CC1114	**High Frequency Picture Words Grades K-1**
CC1115	**Sight & Picture Words Big Book Grades K-1**
CC1100	How to Write a Paragraph Grades 5-8
CC1101	How to Write a Book Report Grades 5-8
CC1102	How to Write an Essay Grades 5-8
CC1103	Master Writing Big Book Grades 5-8
CC1116	**Reading Comprehension Grades 5-8**
CC1117	**Literary Devices Grades 5-8**
CC1118	**Critical Thinking Grades 5-8**
CC1119	**Master Reading Big Book Grades 5-8**
CC1106	Reading Response Forms: Grades 1-2
CC1107	Reading Response Forms: Grades 3-4
CC1108	Reading Response Forms: Grades 5-6
CC1109	Reading Response Forms Big Book: Grades 1-6

MATHEMATICS - Software

ITEM #	TITLE
	PRINCIPLES & STANDARDS OF MATH SERIES
CC7315	Grades PK-2 Five Strands of Math Big Box
CC7316	Grades 3-5 Five Strands of Math Big Box
CC7317	Grades 6-8 Five Strands of Math Big Box

MATHEMATICS - Books

ITEM #	TITLE
	TASK SHEETS
CC3100	Grades PK-2 Number & Operations Task Sheets
CC3101	Grades PK-2 Algebra Task Sheets
CC3102	Grades PK-2 Geometry Task Sheets
CC3103	Grades PK-2 Measurement Task Sheets
CC3104	Grades PK-2 Data Analysis & Probability Task Sheets
CC3105	Grades PK-2 Five Strands of Math Big Book Task Sheets
CC3106	Grades 3-5 Number & Operations Task Sheets
CC3107	Grades 3-5 Algebra Task Sheets
CC3108	Grades 3-5 Geometry Task Sheets
CC3109	Grades 3-5 Measurement Task Sheets
CC3110	Grades 3-5 Data Analysis & Probability Task Sheets
CC3111	Grades 3-5 Five Strands of Math Big Book Task Sheets
CC3112	Grades 6-8 Number & Operations Task Sheets
CC3113	Grades 6-8 Algebra Task Sheets
CC3114	Grades 6-8 Geometry Task Sheets
CC3115	Grades 6-8 Measurement Task Sheets
CC3116	Grades 6-8 Data Analysis & Probability Task Sheets
CC3117	Grades 6-8 Five Strands of Math Big Book Task Sheets
	DRILL SHEETS
CC3200	Grades PK-2 Number & Operations Drill Sheets
CC3201	Grades PK-2 Algebra Drill Sheets
CC3202	Grades PK-2 Geometry Drill Sheets
CC3203	Grades PK-2 Measurement Drill Sheets
CC3204	Grades PK-2 Data Analysis & Probability Drill Sheets
CC3205	Grades PK-2 Five Strands of Math Big Book Drill Sheets
CC3206	Grades 3-5 Number & Operations Drill Sheets
CC3207	Grades 3-5 Algebra Drill Sheets
CC3208	Grades 3-5 Geometry Drill Sheets
CC3209	Grades 3-5 Measurement Drill Sheets
CC3210	Grades 3-5 Data Analysis & Probability Drill Sheets
CC3211	Grades 3-5 Five Strands of Math Big Book Drill Sheets
CC3212	Grades 6-8 Number & Operations Drill Sheets
CC3213	Grades 6-8 Algebra Drill Sheets
CC3214	Grades 6-8 Geometry Drill Sheets
CC3215	Grades 6-8 Measurement Drill Sheets
CC3216	Grades 6-8 Data Analysis & Probability Drill Sheets
CC3217	Grades 6-8 Five Strands of Math Big Book Drill Sheets
	TASK & DRILL SHEETS
CC3300	Grades PK-2 Number & Operations Task & Drill Sheets
CC3301	Grades PK-2 Algebra Task & Drill Sheets
CC3302	Grades PK-2 Geometry Task & Drill Sheets
CC3303	Grades PK-2 Measurement Task & Drill Sheets
CC3304	Grades PK-2 Data Analysis & Probability Task & Drills
CC3306	Grades 3-5 Number & Operations Task & Drill Sheets
CC3307	Grades 3-5 Algebra Task & Drill Sheets
CC3308	Grades 3-5 Geometry Task & Drill Sheets
CC3309	Grades 3-5 Measurement Task & Drill Sheets
CC3310	Grades 3-5 Data Analysis & Probability Task & Drills
CC3312	Grades 6-8 Number & Operations Task & Drill Sheets
CC3313	Grades 6-8 Algebra Task & Drill Sheets
CC3314	Grades 6-8 Geometry Task & Drill Sheets
CC3315	Grades 6-8 Measurement Task & Drill Sheets
CC3316	Grades 6-8 Data Analysis & Probability Task & Drills